Goddess of Ebb and Flow

A Journey to Self- Discovery and Love

By: Evelina Melissae

Raleigh, NC

Copyright © 2021 by Evelina Melissae

All rights reserved. No part of this publication may be reproduced, copied, distributed, or transmitted in any form or by any means, without prior written permission.

Rain Publishing
http://rainpublishing.com

Book Cover Design & Layout: Rain Publishing
Edited by: Lawrence Jones

Goddess of Ebb and Flow – 1st ed.

IBSN: 978-1-7346106-9-7

.

Dedication

I dedicate this book to my Stepfather Robbie Pullen. Thank you for giving me the guts to be myself.

Acknowledgements

My darling husband, you have seen me at my most vulnerable moments and have traveled into the most intimate parts of my heart and mind. Thank you for believing in me when I didn't believe in myself. You have loved and supported me on this exciting journey called life, for that, I am forever grateful.

My sweet mother, thank you for bringing me into this world. The journey of our relationship as mother and daughter has not been easy, but I would not change it for the world. Thank you for listening and accepting me for who I REALLY AM. You are a breath of fresh air with a heart of gold.

My stepfather, pops, although you are no longer physically present on this earth; I know that you are with always me. Despite our short time together, I cherish all the moments I've spent with you. You inspired me to reach for what I wanted and because of you I'm doing just that. The last poem in this book is dedicated to you.

My baby sister, your wisdom inspires me. When I have endured the lowest of low, your words of honesty and truth ground me. You are a beautiful, old soul. I love you dearly and I want you to know it.

I am forever grateful to my spiritual community. Thank you for taking me as I am, still extremely fresh in the journey, but you have remained patient, kind, and understanding with me. Your knowledge and love has seeped deep into my heart. I hope to continue learning and growing with you.

Last, but not least, my divine and gracious God, I thank you for being my comfort and inspiration during the most difficult times of my life. You have taught me what it means to TRULY love myself and embrace my inner magic. I THANK YOU.

Introduction

Did you ever grow up realizing that the path you were taught was the path you could not follow? It only led to a place of deep mental turmoil and self – hatred. I surely did. I have found my greatest comfort in our Divine Mother Earth and learning how to connect with God intimately. I want this to be a sanctuary where others can see themselves and know they are not alone. Life is a journey and a choice all should have. This book is an ode to all who have felt out of place and have forged their own unique path. Let's find your inner holiness and relish in it together.

Introduction

Table of Contents

Chapter 1 The Beginning of the Journey

Thick Rooted Woman

I know a woman that is thick as roots
Strong legs and arms to match
Her heart is just the same
It knows no boundaries
The depth of her is as endless as the oceans
Her stubbornness is a sure fire match
She is tender when she feels it is best
and at times she is sharp like a whip
but heavens knows a woman must BE

Forgive Me My Body

Forgive me my body, my home, my temple.
Forgive me for treating you in unsatisfactory ways.
Forgive me for allowing in enemies who were disguised as friends.
Forgive me for holding on to unnecessary pain and hatred towards you.
Forgive me for allowing society to make me believe that you were never good enough. Forgive me for purging, burning, cutting, and starving you of valid nutrients. Forgive me for not adoring your every roll and crevice. Let me embrace you with my small hands wrapped around your thick roots. Allow me to accept you for all that you are.
But most of all my gorgeous friend, forgive me for thinking you were a delicate flower, when you were a deep, thick, oak with breathtaking textured bark.

The Experiment of Kindness

Have you ever heard of the experiment where a scientist
Took plants and began watering them as normal?
One group of the plants were uttered lovely words.
Whereas the other group was yelled cruel, hurtful, ones.
So what happened at the end of the study you may ask?
The plants that were encouraged and spoken kind phrases
Were full of life. Where those who were spoken ill towards
Began to droop and rot. Studies have been shown that the same
Applies to all forms of life. So I shall do the same to you my dear.
When you begin to tear yourself down, I will water you with kindness
Until you begin to bloom and rise again.
And that my dear is a wholehearted promise.

Chapter 2 Owning the Process

My Body is a Temple

And if my body is a
Temple I'm reclaiming it as my own
But if you speak with honey on your lips
And offer me libations of your love
I'll drink it until I'm drunk
Your affection is the sweetest ambrosia I know
Caress my back with your hand
And connect my freckles like stars
Our love is divine and let's relish in it

Hearth Keeper to My Inner Fire

I used to find my home in others.
It was an ever growing, consistent journey of loss.
I would sit by their fires to find some inner warmth.
My small hands would cup the intangible force I yearned for.
By the time I had found comfort, it had managed to slip through my
fingers yet again. I used to ask myself. What is wrong with me?
Why am I not worthy of their time and endearment?
I was asking the wrong questions.

I was running away from myself.
Instead of trying to embrace this girl with the golden, brown eyes with
dark underneath. I tried to mask her primal shadow and
give up kindling her fire. Now I embrace my once ungrateful spirit
into her aching body. She has gotten me through days I never thought
I'd survive. And she is my home, my temple, my goddess.
I long to stay her hearth keeper even with the blistering storms caving in.
She is worth it.

I Will Not Apologize for Who I am

I may not be the woman you imagined me to be,
but I do know, I am the woman of my own desires.
I lick the honey from my lips and sip the wine of my own
making. I dance naked in the light of the moonlight.
And pray in my own sacred space.
I take pride in my wild ways.
I am a woman with no apologies and no regrets.
And I won't beg for your forgiveness because
for once I am at peace.

I'm Alive, I'm Alive Damn It

I'm drunk on moonlight and loving by daylight.
I kiss the ground and thank it.
Mother Earth is caressing my fragile frame.
The sun beams radiate their warmth into my skin.
The dew of the grass kisses my toes.
The world is a beautiful place and I belong in it.
I'm alive. I'm alive damn it! And my very existence is enough.
Even if things are hard right now.

Chapter 3 Awareness

My God, I Have Found You

I have never felt the move of spirits and divinity in a stuffy
building. For years, I've longed to feel what others talked about,
"that feeling," where the hairs on your neck stand up
and your stomach swirls.
Your heart is pulsing with excitement,
but calm at the same time.
That deep religious experience where you knew the divine was
there, but those white walls, and bland pews held silence.
And believe me, I tried.
Yet, the minute I stepped into the forest I felt a presence unlike
no other. My heart swelled with a peace I have never known.
My God I have found you.

I Am Starting to Love Her

I am kindling a fire in my belly.
This sure blown passion is heating up in my lungs and it is ready
to ignite. For the first time in a long time everything is right
in the world. The goddess within me is coming through,
and I'm starting to love her.

Your Purpose Is Yours to Define

When are you going to realize that you are not made to be like
someone else? My darling child of the stars and earth,
raise your head. Lift up your heart. Your life is uniquely your own.
You are a kind of the universe.
You alone are enough. You are not made to shine like others.
It's time to step out as the person the heavens knew you could be.
Be bright like you, you beautiful soul.
Rise up and own it.

Taste of the Forbidden Fruit

Hell yes, I ate the fruit, and suckled its seeds.
I licked the juice off my lips and fingers rebelliously.
For once in my life, I wanted to choose something that was mine and
mine alone. Something that thrilled me deep down into my bones.
The choice to live life the way I've always dreamed,
with a crown on my head and power to wield at my command.
And let me tell you freedom never tasted sweeter.

Happiness IS Not Linear

Being happy is not a linear journey
It's something I've been having to realize as of late
There will still be days where your soul will
break even in the best of them
It's what it means to be completely and utterly human

Chapter 4 Prayers and Affirmations

Love is A Prayer Away

When darkness comes my way
may I be reminded:
Love is a prayer away.
Love surrounds me.
Love envelopes me.
Love is me.

A Prayer to the Universe

May my breath be a prayer to the universe
May my voice be lifted to the heavens
May my bones root me deeply into the Mother Earth
And may I know in the depths of this chaos
there will be a moment of stillness

The Divine in Me Honors the Divine in You

The Divine in me honors the divine in you
We are all one in Mother Gaia
My kin, may you feel valid
and whole from the tips of your toes
to the top of your head
Your existence is enough

Angels Surround Me

Celestial kisses sent from above
Comfort that feels like a mother's love
Heavenly arms to guide my way
As I go on throughout my day
Angels are with me everywhere
Filling me with peace and tender care

I am the Key

I want to be free of my worries
I want to be free like the rain
That washes over me
I want to feel its deep cleansing powers
Soothing my anguished soul
I want to be rooted like the trees
Deeply planted in the Earth below me
I am the one who holds the key
Only I can let it be

A Wild Woman's Prayer

Oh God of all holy and wild
It is I your daughter
Your feisty child with a tender heart
Mangled hair and teeth sharp
Your undomesticated kind
I bow to your gracious being
I want to thank you for loving me and
Constantly reminding me that I am worthy
Just as I am -SELAH

You are Magic

Goddess sweet as nectar
Hips as thick as honey
Your radiant eyes and skin to match
I stand in awe of your eternal beauty
I crumble in the minute
I behold your glory
Getting hit with this magic and damn
Honey, you're killing it!

An Affirmation from Pops

Resilient one be brave in everything you do
Take every single day one at a time
Know that with each steady breath
The days will begin to get easier
Maybe not at first
The longer things go on
the pain will become lighter
It will take form in a shape
You will be able to finally carry
Then you will be able to move on

About the Author

Wild woman, daughter, sister, wife, and poet are a few of the many hats I wear in my life. To be honest, I am just a woman on a quest to be my most authentic self, as I pursue self-love and empowerment; the battle of mental health and self-esteem wages within me daily. I find peace in the process of growing and changing one day at a time. Truly my spiritual path is a comfort and the foundation for my mental, physical, and spiritual healing. I pray you find your peace as you read this collection of poems.

www.ingramcontent.com/pod-product-compliance
Lightning Source LLC
LaVergne TN
LVHW010548100826
845148LV00013B/2662

* 9 7 8 1 7 3 4 6 1 0 6 9 7 *